OH MERCY

Books by James Goertel

Self Portrait

poems

(2013)

With No Need for a Name

poems

(2012)

Each Year an Anthem

poems

(2012)

Carry Each His Burden

stories

(2011)

Oh Mercy

JAMES GOERTEL

Contents

OH MERCY

~ poems of devotion and doubt ~

2015

for Elaine Frances Goertel

The poems of Oh Mercy were forged from faith
and inspired by the songs of Bob Dylan.

NEW MORNING

New morning wakes the world,
wipes clean transgressions...
of time lost only to time,

saved
only in the bruise and guilty blush
of sunsets,

in the dim, shamefast light
cast by evening stars
slinking slowly and further away from

our prayers, our penance,
our impatience with
today, tomorrow,

and the numbered dawns
with their finite, crepuscular
wash of forgiveness.

SLOW TRAIN COMING

Ghosts come limping
across the lake,

smoke lips pursed,
humming suggestions

of a sere and antediluvian landscape
left behind,

now a strangle of
telephone wires which carry no words

for babies born dead
but smiling,

their doll eyes
fixed on a heaven sagging beneath

the weight of querulous saints
quoting false prophets,

of prostitutes
dressed as priests,

of infidels in exodus
following the sound of thunder,

the fragrance of rain
falling through apparitions,

through the fog
following us all, hovering above the water,

held at bay beyond the window,

but swallowing us whole in our sleep

until shaken awake
by the rattle,

the revenant
of a slow train coming.

GONNA CHANGE MY WAY OF THINKING

Coming to understand

there is a light

which will extinguish

itself

without benefit of wind,

lips turning blue,

pale skin turning cold

as air

abandons a room

holding a still shadow

and the grace

of the loved

to go on

with only faith

to light the way.

SOLID ROCK

Hands of clay grasping, clawing
the curvature of solid rock

despite the repeated stoning
and lack of repentance;

still pushing a boulder away
from an empty tomb.

IN THE GARDEN

Captured
at the cross,
taken hostage
at Calvary,
given life
after living a life
of an eye for an eye,
a tooth for a tooth,
snakebit and embittered,
once betrayed in the garden,
but redeemed at Golgotha.

DEAD MAN, DEAD MAN

In the gray comfort of

purgatory, he sits alone;

apart and away from

men and women biding time,

waiting on the gate;

men and women

neither alive nor dead,

neither saved nor condemned;

unconcerned with the him

or the blood on his hands;

never noticing

his contented grin

at being in between

above and below, though

inside his heart

still swinging from the bent branch

of a Cercis siliquastrum,

the salt of Christ's skin still on his lips.

WHEN YOU GONNA WAKE UP

Night fell
waiting on dawn's dew
to baptize
a new day,
the rock rolled away
to reveal
I too fell asleep.

ARE YOU READY

To stand naked
between the stars,
the scars of the flesh
bathed in their light,
old skin shed
and left to wither
in the garden.

DO RIGHT TO ME BABY (DO UNTO OTHERS)

Seduce me, I dream only your name,
its three syllables
rolling like lullabies
across this tongue
as I talk myself
to sleep,
cursing martyrs
walking the daylight
that remains,
dusk clamoring
to cover these eyes,
my hands finding
only one another
in a prayer for the living and the dead.

SAVING GRACE

The wine

turned back to water,

a saving grace

we could not refuse

walking along alone to Calvary,

following shadows

which slunk with the sun,

our shoulders golden,

but burdened,

the two of us carrying

our guilt

to a hill holding up three crosses,

running with the blood

of forgiveness,

the sacrament

of sacrifice,

the cup filled with neither

wine nor water

which could not pass.

COVENANT WOMAN

Waiting on a woman,

though she has been here

all along, before

in this house built from silent struggle

waiting for hammered resolve,

has left her prayers as alms

though this not a church

waiting on a pilgrimage,

no wanderer's refuge

waiting to grace us both with its sanctimonious sanctuary,

but a simple structure

waiting only on a woman, on a man to fashion a home from faith.

THIEF ON THE CROSS

There he is,

there I am

and there is no difference

between the sun at dusk,

the sun at dawn -

blood, rose, bruise, violet

paint the sky the same,

dawn about to birth

the brand new day,

dusk about to bury its remains

along with us both one day

beneath our labored last breaths.

PRESSING ON

Fashion wisdom
from solid rock
unwilling to move,
waiting for mortal hands
to let go, to take up
four cardinal virtues,
to let go
seven deadly sins,
to take up
three graces;
the burden of brothers,
sisters, sinners, and saints
ameliorated
along the way on a path
through a wilderness
of the heart,
pressing on
past Calvary,
beyond a star
in the east.

YE SHALL BE CHANGED

Eat the flesh which holds the soul bound;
drink the blood drowning the spirit
of humble servants and their patron saints
in the same suffocated breath;
be changed, wash the dust,
every grain of sand from bare feet,
shake the devil from broad shoulder;
nothing and no one can follow now.

PRECIOUS ANGEL (I BELIEVE IN YOU)

She, her,
a woman
weaving salvation
from the prayers
of him, he
who has knelt
beside a marriage bed,
laid himself
prostrate
before her, she
who has made a rosary
of his cast stones,
a catechism
of his kisses
from adust, athirst lips
which whispered her name
for forty days,
pushing its sacred calligraphy
into the wind
to be writ upon the sand
as a supplication,
in atonement
for trespasses
she has forever forgiven,
for denying her
three times
before dawn met the desert
he wandered, a wasteland
fashioned
by him alone.

TRUE LOVE TENDS TO FORGET

Walk on
is all she can do,

damnation following
for a distance

before becoming but a memory
her blue eyes squint to see,

though her heart's hushed beat
has not forgotten,

keeps as a thrum
hummed song

she may sing,
but never does.

WEDDING SONG

Everybody's changing partners
below the swoon and sway

of a pagan moon
above the dizzy spin of music

moving only feet
but never stirring the soul,

when all I want is
your hand in mine,

for you to dance
me across the River Jordan

and off to sleep
for an eternity in your arms.

LOVE MINUS ZERO/NO LIMIT

Embrace the sun of the son

and place it in your heart,

the lovers that have left you

cannot touch you now,

cannot part the clouds

which have come between

the rain of their romance

and love's unconditional love.

I DREAMED I SAW ST. AUGUSTINE

Kiss the feet of the dead,
saints among them;
your breath breathes life
into the chalk bones of infidels,
the charred marrow of martyrs,
me among them;
wakes men from their dreams
of death to walk beside you,
no longer asleep
in the Devil's arms,
nor alone in the somnolence
of eternal perdition.

WHAT CAN I DO FOR YOU?

And he opened his mouth saying,
What can I do for you?
And I opened my heart answering,
What can I do for you?

For blessed are we
who have walked in
darkness,
the light unseen
beneath footsteps
leading the way
to a song
sung in harmony
between the living and the dead,
both deciding
to cast stones no more,
to cast fate to the wind,
to cast doubt to the depths,
to cast nets
from boats blindsided by tempests,
from humble vessels teeming
with shaken apostles and unsure saints
praying their feet will find
solid rock beneath them
one last time,
praying their path to final judgment is walked
in the company of his shadow,
in the company of his voice saying,

What can I do for you?
and answered with a modest echo of
What can I do for you?
from the mouths of whilom infidels.

WHEN HE RETURNS

Blood on the cross,
fall to your knees
and bear witness
below his bare, scarred feet.

Belief is a burden,
carry what you can
and place sin
between his bare, scarred feet.

Betrothed to this world,
divorce yourself from doubt
and beg forgiveness
beneath his bare, scarred feet.

Born a mortal beggar,
fashion alms from faith
and offer prayers
before his bare, scarred feet.

EVERY GRAIN OF SAND

Days numbered

from birth to death

and counting down,

carved into the forgiving wood

of a cross

we carry across

a desert's sands

which hold our fragile footprints

but a moment

on the way to eternity,

every grain

a reminder of our mortality

in this impermanent world,

this finite life.

GOTTA SERVE SOMEBODY

Rummaging
the far reaches of a psyche

held captive,
held hostage

by a material world
in servitude only to itself;

rescuing myself
from the half-truths

of mirrors reflecting
an incomplete portrait;

the spirit
occasioning the frame,

the soul in absentia
for the better part of five decades

and never once
materializing

to heed the Holy Ghost's call
until now.

I AND I (YOU ANGEL YOU)

Thin-faced, hollow-eyed
portraits of our pagan love

I and I, you angel you
stumbling into frame

A picture, a poem,
a prophecy

Lines, lives blurring
beneath a decade's worth of weather

My unknown Native blood
blossoming one last time inside you

Words we spoke lost,
postcards found

Bismarck, San Francisco,
Philadelphia, Rochester

Long walks with patron saints
in Sodom and Gomorrah

A church built in three days,
wrecking ball meets flesh

Ancestors smoking in Polaroids
where no one cheated death

Fat and happy,
skinny, sad memories in a shoebox

French kissing

no longer tastes of youthful summers

Locust song
and the cry of a hawk held in a heart

Baby teeth beneath the pillow
gnawing at a Siamese history

Lightning bugs
carry our memories

Faith swims the length
of a man-made lake

Fathers, mothers, friends
asleep in baptismal wells of mud

The sign of the cross
in a spiritual Las Vegas

Bury us both
with a rabbit's foot and a prayer

ON A NIGHT LIKE THIS

The hush of stars

I feel your pierced hand
reach through

Touch shoulder
Touch sinner
Touch soul

I feel your calm presence
whist within

The hush of heaven

TRYING TO GET TO HEAVEN

Seeing
his hand

In bright bloom
In dead leaf

In bitter root's
taste upon a tongue

Which had not dared
to whisper his name in broad daylight

Which only sighed its two syllables
in prayers confided to the night

Stars held up by branches
Flowers held down by graves

Dead on my feet
until now

No longer asleep
in the garden

Awake and taking note of
the smallest of buds

Spring rife
with resurrection

Limb ascending limb
trying to get to heaven

PAY IN BLOOD

Blood in my eyes

Walk west into a sun cut in half
again and again

Follow roadcuts, cries, and faith toward Calvary
Sleep through the heat of the day

Night hides my infidel footsteps,
the scars of original sin's self mutilation

Blood in my mouth

Cut out my tongue,
preserving the names of my unborn children

Heaven holds them hostage just over the horizon
Stars' cold light cannot stanch sanguine lips

Dawn of the third day fails to arrive,
denying time's salve for self-flagellation

COVER DOWN, BREAK THROUGH

Though our spirits lie under siege,
forgive and forget
those who murdered faith
while we lay
together
in a marriage bed,
praying for rain to fall
from a compassionate sky
burning red with fire,
upon denigrated streets
running red with blood,
to wash away
our own transgressions
of false pride
flushing our faces
and covetous lust
bringing a blush
to cheeks
we should be turning
beneath mortal masks,
letting at last
our cover down,
our souls break through
the barricades
between spirit and salvation
we constructed
while faith lay dying
out in the streets, inside our hearts,
the blood of Christ on our hands.

MOST OF THE TIME

Most of the time
the old man inside of me
can no longer outrun his soul,

desires a dark room
where thoughts are free
to move among the stars,

wants a good woman
to know his heart
is a fragile thing

which remembers more than
she believes,
is but a glass bulb

blown from her lips,
filled with her warm breath,
absent its own blood,

beats a hollow drum
beneath a chest no longer
lifting, falling, lifting, falling

in defiance of death
to fill a life
with sheer bravado

now become but a conflation
of first breath's
desperate gasp to simply survive

and the numbered breaths left
astrology cannot know,
nor alchemy can change

for the old man inside of me
shuffling back and forth
across the length of the attic floor

above this bedroom,
rummaging moldered, cardboard boxes
for Kierkegaard, King James, and Gibran

to make sense of what is left
as I dream below
in only broken English or mise-en-scène,

adding just
meaningless narrative and jump cuts
to an incomplete catechism

written partly
in the sun christened, godforsaken hours
of day after day, decade after decade,

partly in the dark of devil-may-care sleep
where I startle awake saints
to ask them my name,

uncertain anymore
and waking myself shaken, unsatisfied,
and unable to remember their answers

and left with only
the three same childhood prayers
to plead for one more day

with a good woman
who, like I, is but flesh and bone,
her face as aged as mine,

but her heart still beating
strong enough for both of us
most of the time.

IT TAKES A LOT TO LAUGH, IT TAKES A TRAIN TO CRY

Train whistle
following my footsteps out of Galilee,
smoke shuttering a Nazarene sky
and the only star
which can carry me
to the end of the line,
back to the beginning
before I am abandoned by my father,
before I find myself motherless,
cast out of a kingdom
built from a cradle
and a faith born
of a woman
walking to Bethlehem,
to Golgotha
to the sound of Gabriel's horn
blowing
to announce a savior's birth,
to lament a son's Passion,
to decree death to be a new beginning
waiting at the end of the line,
beyond the stations of the cross.

THE LEVEE'S GONNA BREAK

The river
cutting, carving,
concealing a path to salvation

Stones carried,
but not our sins,
into an ocean unforgiving

Flooding banks
with holy water
which cannot be damned

The levee
built by man's hubris
breaking in the wake of mortality

TEMPEST

Quintus
nowhere to be found
and lingering with death

Beneath a snakebit tempest
raining over his head

Upon venom-soaked grass
hissing at his heels

Below an ironclad cloud
barring his asp soul

Nicodemus
nowhere to be found
at the hour of his death

LONG AND WASTED YEARS

Dragging this bottomless night
with nothing to medicate
a mind but nicotine
and snippets
of scripture
I piece together from a memory
splintered by desire sleeping
where love once lay
and I am ashamed
of prayers
offered for selfish purpose,
devoid of
genuine sentiment
or a sense of humility
to balance drunken invocations
seeking flesh, squandering
spirit on puerile cupidity
night after night,
filling a soul
with the black water
I now drag for lost time
between baptism and benediction.

WHEN THE NIGHT COMES FALLING FROM THE SKY

Gospel songs
from the throat
of this sinner
escaping the dusk,

haunting the hearts
of dead lovers
who have breached
Heaven's walls

to lie in the arms
of martyred saints
and misguided angels
swaying in communion

to the mortal hum
among the living
condemned to sing
their way back home

through the dark
clutching only hymnals
and the cold hands
of the damned.

ONE OF US MUST KNOW (SOONER OR LATER)

Confessing to myself

that as good as I have been,

I have been but half a man

wandering a wasteland

of my own making,

the agnostic sun masking

The Maker's face,

sand in my eyes, arid wind

chapping lips

which only mumbled

self serving prayers,

a mirage of me

speaking in tongues

but never asking for forgiveness

on a quixotic pilgrimage

to Ponce de Leon's *Fountain of Youth*

ending instead at Gethsemane.

WHERE TEARDROPS FALL

Wipe the tears from your face, mother,

with the *Shroud of Turin,*

with the cloth which wrapped

the body of your son;

gather your family

under tongues of flame

in the twilight

of a new day

dawning without him

and cry no more outside a tomb

where teardrops fall

upon dust to dust

to make a mud,

a balm, a salve, an unguent

to soothe the sting of loss.

ALL THE TIRED HORSES

Soft glow,
the warm, rubicund blood of Christ
bleeding a horizon of its unforgiving glare
from a sun which blinded even the eyes of God
to our idle hands which whipped all the tired horses
we were asked by him to simply water, feed, and shelter
at sundown.

A HARD RAIN'S A-GONNA FALL

The world is burning

but I go to bed

just the same,

pray for a hard rain

to wash away

the blood on the ground

at Golgotha,

but not

to extinguish the flame

of Pentecost.

SIGN ON THE CROSS

With a mouth full of clouds

my own words are lost on me

and so, because it is so,

I carry on

continuing

to make the sign of the cross,

to talk with God

who understands my tongues

which speak in shameful tones

and spitting curses,

ask for forgiveness

and the strength to carry on

in the shadow of his son

parting dark clouds

with *Father, forgive them*

sighed beneath a sign on the cross.

BEYOND THE HORIZON

In a dream, not a dream,
I could not say goodbye;
I could not return to the woods,
a garden of maple, spruce, and pine
behind a house
which still stands
but has not seen my shadow
in nearly a half century,
which held the dreams and desires
of a child who could not account
for time
which took its own sweet time
to shake a man awake
to a life beyond the horizon
where science and spirituality
sleep in the same bed,
dreaming to be born again,
to say hello to Heaven
while waving goodbye to all I have known,
no longer asleep
and unaware
of another man's suffering
for the sake of the unborn.

I FEEL A CHANGE COMIN' ON

Outrunning ourselves at last
through rushes, field, and thicket,

Arms scarred
from never having slowed down,

Not even for
the narrow mountain passes,

There, toward the end
when we were at our most exhausted,

But on the verge
of being reborn and about to change,

Our feet free
to run on beyond ourselves again,

But never again without Him,
He whose feet were nailed to a cross.

LO AND BEHOLD

We relied on instinct,

followed the years of smoke

and falling leaves to St. Gregory;

fell to our knees

in exhaustion, in exultation,

in humble recognition

of the stumbling, secular path

taken through this rocky world

to salvation

from the struggle between

devotion and doubt,

from ourselves.

JOKERMAN

The many faces he wears,

the mask that looks

like mine

My hand

painting him into the picture

painted at others' expense

My hand

in his hand and laughing

in the face of mankind

The many faces we wear,

the mask that looks

like his

HOUSE CARPENTER

Considering Joseph, humble carpenter,
entrusted to see the temple built,
only to see it torn down and built again
in three days' time, I should, must, shall
assume his shadow and walk, head bowed,
into the house of God built from the light
of a new morning, the bones of his only begotten
son, and upon a foundation of unwavering faith.

TOO MUCH OF NOTHING

Fill your hands

with riches like water

slipping through your fingers

and on to an ocean

swallowing

all that withers,

all that rusts,

all that turns to stone

including the hearts

which beat, but do not believe

inside an empty vessel.

WE BETTER TALK THIS OVER

Oh mercy, the aimless hours

we spent discussing, debating

the meaning, the message -

an endless one-sided palaver

of the intellect which never

thought to query

the heart, the soul -

life's litany like a series

of prayers seemingly unanswered.

But, oh mercy,

how wrong were we -

listening at last

and hearing

with more than our ears

the comfort of

His conversation

which has always

been there.

TEARS OF RAGE

And Moses parted the sea
for the chosen fleeing Pharaoh's army
before infidels nailed our Lord to the cross
and black rain, tears of rage fell from a crying sky
to mix with His blood in sanguine streams
making the journey to the Jordan River
and the sea Moses parted.

APPLE SUCKLING TREE

She tempts me,

limbs laden with apples

sway above her head,

her hand reaches

and pulls red flesh

into the pink of her soft palm,

pushes the fruit

of sin, of mortality

into my waiting mouth

and I am

forever changed

and living among

the dead men walking to damnation

until I reach

for the forgiveness

He offered from a cross.

ONE MAN'S LOSS

Sway
with the congregation
or go your own way,

make your path
through the pain
to the promise,
to the joy,

but please
remember,
do keep in mind,

temptation is but a shadow
beyond a shoulder,
lingers behind
the blink of an eye

waiting to betray
one man's loss
in the name of salvation

for the man yet to be born
and still not promised by fate
nor by faith
to either the pain or the joy.

SOMETHING'S BURNING, BABY

Without these doubts
devotion is just smoke
without the penance of fire,
poor Lazarus left to lie
with the dead despite Jesus' tears
along with our own
untested lives, buried alive
without burning to believe.

OBVIOUSLY FIVE BELIEVERS

Cast out among outcasts

to ford a waterless river,

to cross a sea of sand

to find Daniel waiting by the wall

blowing dust from what is written,

what is told: the Kingdom of God

welcomes the humble of heart.

I THREW IT ALL AWAY

Fleeing
a room on fire
built from
sticks
and arrogance

Freeing
a murder of crows
from a heart
made of blood-red
brick and carrion

Giving
up the ghost
of gold spun from straw
in exchange
for forgiveness

I'M NOT THERE

Looking for me,
though they won't find me
inside this skin
which until this moment
seemed so familiar,
the rouge of family blood
once warm beneath
but now gone
to lie with the dead
wandering below
the place of the skull
where one man gave his life,
his flesh, his forgiveness
for the lost flock
this pale infidel followed
until dawn found me,
bathed me
in a baptism of new light
across old skin
shed at last
and leaving only a memory,
the faded tattoo of mortality
for those I left behind
to discover.

CRY A WHILE

A song sung into my heart
by parched lips
split beneath a profane sun

which cast
the shadow of a cross
across

the clotted ground of Calvary
where two Marys cried
in perfect counterpoint.

YOU AIN'T GOIN' NOWHERE

Linger, languish outside the light,
vulture eyes look down
upon the living dead

from parapets of Gothic cathedrals,
shadow structures swallowed
by a night without end

where within our prayers linger,
languish, are at the mercy of
Apollyon's birds of prey.

KNOCKIN' ON HEAVEN'S DOOR

Brother slew brother
under a cold sun,
birds fell from branches,
their song suffocated
by the blood of
jealousy, the asphyxia of anger;
their flight from nest to clouds
brought down to earth;
their wings gathered
by a bitter, bereaved wind
in an offering
to a slain son
buried beneath
trees barely able to hold
their own shadows
while reaching for Heaven.

MAN OF PEACE

Soldier, sailor, and death-defier

with a soul

sewn from the cloth

of a hem

from a holy garment

stained with the salt of the earth.

ONE MORE NIGHT

Stop
the world
with one hand,

Light
a match
with the other.

All is darkness
despite the
sun.

DAY OF THE LOCUSTS

For seventeen years
I wandered,
a snake in either hand,
a hissing wind at my heels,
face turned away from the sun,
lips parted to pray
but all that escaped
for a decade and seven
was a mouthful of sand,
not a man from mortality.
The weight of the world
shed just one grain at a time,
the burden of conscience,
trouble in mind like a crown of thorns,
worn,
carried across a desert of the soul
to kiss the face of Jesus weeping,
to suckle the blood, the tears from his cheek.

SAVED

Take my hand,

the sea has been parted

and we walk on through the misty remains

of a tempest,

The air about us

moist with birdsong

and kissed by light pouring from a heaven

we abandoned

To find one another

hand in hand in mortal bliss

well after our births, long before our deaths

separate us.

DOWN IN THE FLOOD

Sweet child baptize me

for I am old and friendless,

sitting quietly watching the rain

throw coins into the river

which offers no forgiveness

to the valley below,

nor to any man

who cannot wait on redemption,

who cannot reach high ground,

who can only

call for holy water,

call for firewater;

hoping to be

saved in one or drowned in the other

but going down in the flood

despite a man's best efforts to fortify

not a body but a soul.

CRASH ON THE LEVEE

I am cast out,
thrown against the rocks
piled high to hold back the rushing waters
of a river I have swum for years
against the current;
my faith, ragged and torn,
headed downstream beside a soul
flooded with doubt,
devotion dashed upon a broken barricade
between me and my Maker.

NOTHING WAS DELIVERED

Drag faith by the heels,

burn the cross,

bloody the noses

of saints wandering streets

with signs

warning of the end

and pray not to die again,

but go kicking and screaming

when death does come

if Heaven is only

a fable of fabulists

whose bones are but dust,

whose bible is carried

into the coffin

by cold hands

counting on

Christ's own hour of doubt

to comfort souls

about to be commended.

DRIFTER'S ESCAPE

I listened at the river

but could not hear His name

whispered by the wind

through swaying reeds

along the banks,

water on the brink

of leaving its path to an ocean

swallowing all sound

beneath its waves

where I have waded

waiting to be washed ashore,

to lie in the sands of so much

that has come before me

which has passed

into silence,

where I will put a shell

to my ear

one final time

to listen to the sea beyond me,

but will hear instead His words

coming in waves

to this drifter,

to comfort me, to forgive me

for wandering the length

of so many rivers

without ever hearing

His name upon the wind

through swaying reeds

along the banks.

LAY LADY LAY

Lie with me here a while,

the shadows on the ceiling

are the silhouettes

of all I have forsaken,

the sullen reflections

of godless thoughts

and pagan beliefs

which have laid me low,

which haunt my dreamless sleep,

which have made a martyr

of the days I took all

He has given me for granted,

including you.

LORD PROTECT MY CHILD

I am a stumble of skin and bones

breathing the dust of Golgotha,

uncertain of my fate

but speaking in tongues

understood

as I make a pilgrimage

of the path between birth and death

with only one final wish

offered to a wind

which has swept across Calvary

since a son

sacrificed all for the sake

of a sinner like me

who asks not for salvation,

but only, *"Lord, protect my child."*

OH MERCY

Oh mercy

Walk tall through life
while still learning how to crawl

Oh mercy

Bow down on bended knee
while still learning how to pray

About the Author

Born in North Dakota, James Goertel spent twenty years working in television for ABC, NBC, and ESPN among others. His writing has appeared in Ascent Aspirations, Manifold, LucidPlay, NexTV, The Quivering Pen, The Writer's Handful, Yareah Magazine, The Next Best Book Club, and Short Story America. His short fiction has been published in anthologies by Rod Serling Books and Short Story America Press. Much of his poetry has been serialized by Yareah Magazine in Madrid, Spain.

Acknowledgements

This collection is dedicated to my mother, Elaine Frances Goertel. Her faith in me has been my church and her strength and love my bible.

This collection owes a debt to Bob Dylan, the first poet I became aware of and the one I find myself returning to again and again.

And with Gratitude

Thank you to Dr. Rachel Adams Goertel and Henry Goertel for their support and love and to my father, Donald Goertel, whose faith was a quiet example and whose writing remains an inspiration. Most of all thank you to those who read my work.

OH MERCY

JAMES GOERTEL

...and I'm trying to get to Heaven before they close the door...

~ Bob Dylan

Made in the USA
Coppell, TX
04 November 2022